Magical Stories for Kids

Short Stories for Children to Help Their Imagination.

Sarah Mindfulness

Thanks to the simple narrative nuclei and situations, this book offers the opportunity to listen to stories designed and written for children aged 6 to 9 years.
Short stories to let the imagination fly.

Legal & Disclaimer

Table of Contents

THE WITCH PRISCILLA

In a thick wood on the edge of the countryside, inside a small cave, lives the witch Priscilla.

Today is her birthday and she has invited wizards and witches for a big party. Make spaghetti with a sauce made from garlic, lettuce, acorns, mushrooms, turtle eggs and tender cobwebs. To toast, prepare a liqueur made from pine needles.

Weave garlands of lilies of the valley and cyclamen to decorate her cave.

When everything is ready he calls her friends. They form a nice circle around a fire and sing all night long. All of Priscilla's friends love going to her parties.

PIRATES AT SEA

The female pirate Elsa looks at the sea. There is so much to discover: flying fish, dolphins doing stunts and even an island can be glimpsed in the distance.

Elsa leans forward with curiosity, but suddenly a wave crashes against the ship and knocks the pirate into the sea. -

Help! - Elsa clings to a branch floating on the water.

The other two pirates are unable to hear Elsa's requests for help and leave with the ship. Elsa is terrified: something is touching her leg. Will it be a shark?

A turtle floats next to her.

-Jump on! - the animal offers her kindly, - I'll take you to the island!

The journey to the island passes quickly: Elsa is enchanted to watch the colorful fish swimming in the clear water.

- I'd like to give you something to thank you, - Elsa says to the turtle as soon as they reach the island.

- Unfortunately, however, all my things are on the ship, which is now gone.

- Turn around a bit! - suggests the turtle, laughing under his mustache. Elsa can't believe her eyes: her ship is just a few steps away!

- Hi Elsa! - her pirate friends shout as they walk towards her. Then they hug happily.

Elsa runs aboard the ship to pick up her most beautiful hat.

- Thank you! - replies the turtle, immediately trying on the hat. Then all together celebrate Elsa's rescue.

THE TREASURE HUNT

Today is a special day: the king has organized a treasure hunt to amuse everyone who works for him.

All knights can participate in the game and share the loot.

- I'll be the one to find the treasure! - Casimiro says to himself. But he overslept, damn it!

He jumps out of bed and hits his helmet.

- Ugh! As usual! - he sighs, getting angry at the dent on the helmet.

It is now late. Casimiro hurries: he absolutely wants to go in search of the treasure and gets dressed quickly.

Horses can be heard galloping from outside. The treasure hunt has already begun and he is forced to skip breakfast. Casimiro rushes into the courtyard of the castle, but there is no one left. Then he runs into the stable: but the horses are no longer there.

There is only one donkey left. What a misfortune!

Casimiro a little resigned gets on the donkey and heads into the woods, with his stomach rumbling with hunger. He hears screams: it is the other knights who are coming back.

- The treasure is lost forever! - the knights complain. - A dragon stole it!

Casimiro would like to go back with the others, but his donkey continues and goes straight to the dragon!

Casimiro is afraid! The dragon guards the chest, but as soon as he sees Casimir, he starts laughing.

- What a funny knight! - he chuckles. - With a dented helmet and riding a donkey! So funny!

Casimiro also has to laugh, while his belly continues to grumble.

- The noise of your stomach is louder than my roar! - exclaims the dragon.

- But don't worry, I have something for both of us. Look in the chest for a while.

Casimiro is on cloud nine: he is full of chocolates!

- Thank you, dear dragon, they were very good! - shouts Casimiro.

The rest he takes away with him to give to the other knights. He can't wait to share the treasure with them.

- See you soon! - promises his new friend when he leaves.

THE WINGED DRAGON

One day a winged dragon was sighted flying over Peropoli because he was lost. Fly here and fly there, by now he had lost his energy.

At one point he was forced to ring the door of a house because he was hungry and needed food: a child opened the door and, taken by amazement and fright, closed the door immediately and ran to his room.

The dragon, in turn astonished by the child's reaction, rang the door again for an explanation. The child took courage and opened it again.

This time he found the strength to ask him what he wanted and the dragon replied: - I would like some food, because I have been flying for a long time and I am hungry!

The quieter child went into the kitchen and returned with a loaf of bread which he prepared to deliver to the dragon, who ate it in one gulp.

The grateful dragon greeted the child and flew back to his home.

THE DESIRE

This story is the story of a slightly spoiled princess who always expects the impossible.

-No! - Princess Mira cried, -I don't like stripes, I want a checkered zebra! The groom, who knew the princess's wish well, sighed: - Your Highness, checkered zebras don't exist!

But the princess wanted to know: - Bring me a checked zebra by tonight!

Otherwise I will look for another groom.

The groom thought about it all night and couldn't help but paint some black squares on a white pony. In the evening, the princess returned to the stables and was delighted to find a checkered zebra!

But what would she come up with the next day? Every day Princess Mira would come up with a different request: once she wanted a pink and red cake. Another day he asked for purple finned goldfish.

One fine day, however, the princess couldn't think of anything to ask, not even a small wish. - I absolutely must find something to wish for - said the princess. She decided to go for a carriage ride. On the way he met a little girl.

- My name is Sara - she said - I can't find my Tigger dog. Have you seen it by any chance?

- Unfortunately not - answered the princess - but at least now I know what my wish is today: that you can find your dog.

Mira ordered all the knights of the kingdom to go in search of Tigger. The princess and Sara searched for him on foot. Mira then understood what she had always lacked: a friend. Finally a knight managed to find the dog. Tigger was lost in the woods.

-Thank you very much- said Sara who was really really happy.

- Will we meet again soon? - asked Princess Mira.

- Of course - cried Sara - if you want tomorrow too!

Princess Mira was happy and for the first time in her life she had nothing more to ask for.

HOW THE STARFISH WAS BORN

Many years ago, not far from the sea, some elephants lived: an elephant was giant, an elephant was large, an elephant was medium, an elephant was small, and an elephant was small. Elephants looked at the stars every night and dreamed of playing with them.

One night the giant elephant proposed to catch one and, said and done, took the big elephant by the trunk and loaded it on its back. The big elephant caught the medium elephant in the air and so did the small elephant and the little elephant.

The little elephant holding its breath, stretched out its trunk and managed to catch a little star. From the emotion of the little elephant, a tingle in the nose came, he sneezed and the star escaped him falling into the sea.

The next morning, walking slowly, the elephants noticed the star floating on the water and told them:

- Hello, I've become a starfish!
And all the elephants said to the little elephant: - Thank you!

THE MAGIC EXAMINATION

Zimbalo, a wizard apprentice, is very agitated. Tomorrow he must take the magic exam. If he manages to overcome it, he can cast spells even outside the academy: he has been waiting for this moment for a long time.

The problem is, he's still not very good at magic. There is always something that goes wrong.

-Now I have to go, - says his teacher Zambo, - practice well for tomorrow! Trust your abilities!

And waving his magic wand disappears in a moment.
Zimbalo reviews the magic formulas. Suddenly he sees a spider on his book.

What if he tries to transform it? Casting a spell on an animal is very difficult.

The aspiring magician hesitates for a moment. He is alone in the castle: if something goes wrong, no one will be able to help him. But in the end Zimbalo takes courage and says:

- Spider legs and wings of magic, sweet little animal, fly away!

Golden stars appear and instead of the spider there is now a bird.

Zimbalo is very proud: it is the first time he has managed to cast a spell on an animal. But now he wants to make the spider reappear.

- What is the inverse formula like? Ah yes: Feathers and magic, now bird you have to go!

What is happening? Suddenly, there is a whole flock of birds in the room.

Zimbalo must have pronounced the magic formula wrong! Fortunately, the right one immediately comes to mind:
- Birds and stars come here and everything will return as before!

A flash appears and in an instant all the birds disappear. Here is the spider walking blissfully on the spellbook again. Luckily, he did it!

Suddenly Zimbalo hears the voice of his teacher behind him:

-Well done! You passed the exam! Zimbalo turns around in amazement.

- But the exam is tomorrow! - he exclaims, - And where do you come from, so suddenly?

- I never went away, - Zambo says, - I just became invisible so I could examine you without being seen.

- This time too, however, I did something wrong, - admits Zimbalo.

- It's true, - says Zambo, - but it's not that bad, because you trusted yourself and managed to make the spider reappear by yourself. This is what matters! I give you your first wizard's magic wand.

- Does it also work outside the castle walls?

- Sure Zimbalo!

The boy is happy, finally now he is a true magician.

ANDREA AND THE BEAR

Once upon a time there was a curious and brave boy, named Andrea, who loved nature.

One day he decided to climb a very steep and wooded high mountain, to be able to observe the view from above. After a long climb he found a big bear, covered in brown fur, with two angry eyes. The child no longer knew what to do, silently he took refuge in a cave and remained there until morning.

As soon as the sun rose he saw a young eagle that immediately approached him to help him. The eagle made him get on his back, took off and brought Andrea back to the ground. The boy was happy and thanked her.

A FRIEND FOR LUCY

- Hello, how are you? - asks the little dredge Lucy.

The pony approaches and sniffs it with curiosity. Lucy also sniffs the animal, but clouds of smoke come out of the emotion from her nose.

The pony gets scared and runs away galloping. What a pity! Lucy watches him run away with sadness, Lucy would love to have a friend. She cannot understand why most animals are afraid of her: she is the kindest and cutest dragon in the world.

While she was absorbed in these thoughts, Lucy sighs, causing a flash of fire to come out of her nose.

-Clack, clack, clack!- replies an angry stork with its beak and flies away quickly. The flash of fire was about to hit her and burn her feathers!

- Damn! I didn't really see you! - Lucy apologizes. But the stork has already gone away. Sadly, Lucy sits down on a sun-warmed rock.

-Beautiful, is not it? - a voice suddenly asks her. Lucy opens her eyes wide in amazement. Next to her there is a creature she had never seen. It almost seems like a ...

- Are you by any chance a dragon too? - asks Lucy.

-Not really, the creature replies - I am an iguana and my name is Luis.

Luis doesn't get scared when Lucy spits fire with joy. In fact, she loves the heat, just like the dragon!

Lucy and Luis spend the rest of the day together on the rock.

They have so many things to tell each other!

That same evening, Lucy falls asleep happy: finally with Luis, she has found a friend.

NICOLINA, THE MINI GIRL

Nicolina was a little bit special, now I'll tell you why.

She was a small child, but very, very small and it often happened that they lost her.

She lived with his grandparents in a small house on the edge of the woods. Nicolina had remained small because a fairy had cast a spell on her when she was born and she hadn't grown up since. The grandparents loved her very much, but they were terrified of losing her, of accidentally crushing her, of dropping her, she was so small. So the grandmother thought of attaching a chain to her neck with a golden bell, so they could hear it wherever she went.

Over time, however, Nicolina became sadder and sadder, because she could not go to school like the others: it took her almost all morning to go to school and when she was there, how did she write in those giant notebooks? So her grandmother taught her how she could, everything she knew. Her grandfather had arranged to make her a bespoke wooden bedroom, so that the child could have a bed of her size, a small table, a wardrobe just right for her clothes. Despite the efforts of her grandparents, Nicolina was still sad.

She wanted to be free to do everything other children did, she wanted to be able to play with others, she wanted to be free to move around the house without the fear of being crushed by someone.

One day, while the little girl was lost in her thoughts, a pigeon approached her and asked her if she wanted to take a ride with him: to Nicolina it didn't seem real to be able to see the world from above, so she accepted. It was a sensational flight, full of adrenaline!

When the pigeon brought her home she said: - Never, never could I have asked a child to get on top of me for a ride! You are a lucky girl, because thanks to your height you have the possibility to fly with me! If you want, I'll be back to see you soon for another round.

Nicolina had never thought about the luck she had, on the contrary, she had only focused on the disadvantages of being small. So, from that day, she understood that the important thing is to appreciate what you have and take advantage of it, as much as possible.

BIRBINA THE STARFISH

One day Birbina, the starfish who lived on the ocean floor, went for a walk in search of shells. At one point a diver passed by her.

- Who are you? - Birbina asked him.

The diver replied: - I'm a spearfisher and I'm looking for some special fish to sell them and earn some money.

Who are you?

- I'm Birbina. You don't want to take me too, do you? -added the starfish.

- Actually, I would like to take you to my little girl who wants a starfish so much - said the diver.

- Please don't let me die. Put me in a little water then, when your little girl sees me bring me back here to my blue sea- Birbina begged.

The diver promised Birbina that he would take her back to sea. So he put the starfish in a bucket full of water and went home. When the daughter saw her dad come back with a bucket in hand, she ran to meet him: how great was her surprise in seeing what was there inside of! She had never seen a starfish in her life! It was wonderful!

Her father explained that her name was Birbina and the next day he would have to take her back to the sea, as he had promised the starfish.

The day after at dawn, the little girl and the fisherman brought Birbina back to sea and thanked her for being admired. Birbina said goodbye and set off gently carried away by the waves of the sea.

PANDOLFINA AND THE WAVES OF THE SEA

Pandolfina was a very pretty little girl: she had an oval face enlivened by two blue eyes, big and shining like the stars. His body was thin but full of energy. Pandolfina was as cheerful as a bird during the summer: she ran in the meadows, she was affectionate with her companions, generous with everyone, ready to share her things with others.

She loved nature and sometimes she spent hours contemplating the clouds moving in the sky or the grass in the meadow moved by the wind, or the waves of the sea breaking on the shore.

One day she went to the dock and watched the waves make white crests of foam. At a certain moment, a wave larger than the others raised a foam so white and light that Pandolfina was attracted to it; she jumped and ... "Oh" you will say " she drowned".

But no, Pandolfina walked on the crest and since then continues to circle from one wave to another, greeting those who look her.
But you, don't do like her, because Pandolfina was not a child like the others but a fairy, a good fairy of the sea.

THE BLUE SEED

One day Curious Gnome found a seed never seen before in a corner of the garden. It was as big as a hazelnut, blue and unknown.

Curious went to look at his gardening books, but that seed just wasn't there. The job of the seeds, however, is to be planted and sprouted, so Curious dug a big hole and rolled the big blue seed into it.

Then he waited, watering from time to time. Finally the seed sprouted. It became a seedling, then a tall, very tall plant, taller than all the others: strong and robust. It went up, higher and higher. But where was he going?

Curious decided to find out. He climbed, branch by branch. At the top, he looked around: he saw his little little garden below, he saw the world down there; he saw the sky above his head.

-Good blue seed! -he said. - Now I understand why you are blue: because you are like a ladder to the sky!

The blue seed plant is still in the garden.

And whenever Curious wants to touch the sky he goes up, up, up. And he feels happy up there.

DELETE, DELETE

Sofia was drawing a house on a piece of paper. She began to erase and a hole formed in the paper. A little woman came out of the paper and began to complain, because a lot of air was getting in from that hole.

- I'm sorry - Sophie said - but I didn't really do it on purpose.

- Oh well, now do not take it so much, after all when you live in drawings you get used to these things. It would be worse if you had drawn a ship.

- Oh yeah? - Sophie asked. - And why? -Because ships sink and houses don't! - the little woman replied.
- Do you also mean the drawn ships?

- Of course, even those ... I remember once a child drew a ship and then, erase erase, a nice hole came out right on the water, so the ship immediately began to sink!

Luckily that child had also drawn a small island, so those who were on the ship had time to take refuge on it.

THE CORINNA LEAF

Once upon a time there was a very beautiful leaf that belonged to a majestic oak. She felt really important and flaunted her beauty every time the wind blew that made her dance among the foliage.

Autumn also came and you know, in that season the leaves must leave their tree, but Corinna didn't want to know, Corinna would never have left her oak for any reason. Who would have admired it there on the ground, together with all the other leaves?

Every day she remained tenaciously attached to the branch, despite the temperatures becoming increasingly cold and the wind blowing threateningly. The days passed and she was still there, proud of her courage. She was left alone, all her companions had let themselves be detached by the wind friend. A very strong storm also came which put a strain on the leaf, which, by now exhausted, dropped to the ground, tired and demoralized for not having succeeded in its enterprise.

But the next day, a child passing by noticed it: that leaf was really beautiful, he had never seen anything so beautiful and above all it was still green. He could not leave it there among all the other leaves now crushed and moldy from humidity. So he picked it up and took it home. In order not to spoil its beauty, he placed it inside a glass frame, so he could admire it whenever he wanted.

A NEW SISTER

Guido was tired of his little sister Sofia, because she put on airs and was disgusted by lizards and spiders. He then decides to buy a new one.

That afternoon he took his bike and went to the supermarket, the one that sold new brothers. There they had new brothers and sisters and there was cheap quality stuff. On a shelf he saw a six-pack of frozen sisters and put it in the cart, because it was cheap and they even gave you Pokemon figurines.

Beyond was a bank of sisters on sale: some were missing teeth or were too fat. He bought a powdered sister that would take shape in contact with water.

He went home satisfied with his bag and placed everything in the freezer and cupboard. His sister was right there waiting for him and watching him curiously. He was holding a tray of spider and snake cookies prepared for the Halloween party.

Guido felt guilty for all those fake sisters and as soon as night came, he threw all his purchases in the trash and decided to keep his sister as she was.

THE BABY MOUSE TIM GOES INTO SPACE

Tim the mouse is a very curious type, especially when it comes to astronomy: he knows all the names of the planets, the names of galaxies and many constellations.

One day he has an unstoppable desire to go and see everything he was studying up close. By chance he found a flyer on the street that depicted the release of a new film, "Topostellar

Adventures in Space". How many dreams crowd his mind that night!

The following Sunday he decides to go to see the film and with great energy begins to organize his expedition into space, just like the protagonist of the film.

Think and rethink, the first thing to do is make a rocket: get some cardboard tubes and colored paper. Within a few days, everything is ready for its exploration in space. He asks his dad for help to get pushed into space with a thruster and his mom who makes him a spacesuit and a helmet full of stars.

Everything is ready, Tim is full of enthusiasm and concentration. The countdown starts: three, two, one ... Away, Tim is in space and full of amazement looks around: what a wonder, what immensity! Everything seems like magic to him!

With his rocket he goes around the Earth and after thirty minutes he is back at home, full of things to tell! What an exhilarating experience !!!

THE GIFT OF THE DEER

Once upon a time there was a lumberjack who did not know how to feed his family. He was really poor and every night, when he came home to his wife and three children, he would cry.

One day, walking through the woods to retrieve wood, he met a deer who said to him:

- My horns are fairy and have magical powers: if you take off the first piece you can have all the food you need to feed your family, if you take off the second piece you will get weapons and armor, if you take off the third you will get clothes and items precious.

You can only choose one, tomorrow you will go back to the woods and you will come and get the piece of horn you need. As soon as he got home, the lumberjack told his family what had happened.

The wife said: - I want the first one, so we will always have food to feed us!

The male child shouts: - I want the second, so I will become a strong warrior.

The two daughters shouted: -We want the third, so we will be beautiful and elegant!

Soon, the children and his wife began to argue about which horn was the best and although the lumberjack tried to get them together, he could not.

The next morning the lumberjack went back into the woods and told the deer that he would not take any piece of his antlers, because the choice of which piece was the best had led to quarrels, without reaching a solution.

The deer, admired by such honesty, decided to make an exception to the rule and gave all three horns to the lumberjack, who, moved, thanked the animal for its great generosity.

With the three horns the family lived peacefully in abundance and everyone was satisfied.

THE LIGHTHOUSE
GUARDIAN

Peter, the lighthouse keeper, lived on a remote island. He spent his days looking at the sky and the sea. He rarely encountered any ships passing by and even more rarely did the ships stop on the island. Pietro's only task was to turn on the lighthouse at dusk for the passing ships and then he went to bed.

But one evening, seized by inexplicable fatigue, he forgot to turn on the lighthouse and went to bed. He fell into a deep sleep, but during the night he was abruptly awakened: a ship had crashed on the island's reef causing a loud noise of scrap metal. Pietro thought he was dreaming, but the screams of the ship's passengers woke him up for good. He immediately rushed ashore and immediately took action. Thanks to the lifeboats all passengers were safe and Pietro took care of everyone with extreme generosity for a few days, until the ship was repaired. At the time of saying goodbye, Peter was sad, but so happy for the adventure he had experienced and the passengers thanked him warmly.

Even today, from time to time, some passengers on the ship visit Pietro at the lighthouse.

A ALL CRAZY PENCIL

Mina was a crazy pencil because it didn't act like a pencil at all. From the very first day it was made and taken to a downtown stationery to be sold, it had shown signs of madness. Mr.

Sergio, a highly experienced stationer, always found Mina out of the jar of pencils. One day he even found all the pencils on the ground. In fact, Mina had tried to escape and wanted to go around the city.

One day Marco came to the shop and bought it with the material for the start of school. He chose Mina because it seemed to him that it was more lucid than the others, it seemed almost alive! The special pencil did not miss the opportunity to show its uniqueness: it slipped between books and notebooks, punctured the envelope that contained it and ended up among Marco's toys. The research of the pencil was useless, because Mina was having so much fun among Lego, toy cars and plastic animals. Marco resigned himself to asking his mother for a new pencil, while Mina was hiding all day between toys.

But one day, the mother started cleaning Marco's room: that's where the pencil they bought had gone! So she put it on the desk for her son to see, but when Marco came back from school, the pencil had disappeared again. This time Mina, for fear of being discovered and caged in a pencil case, had taken the direction of the window and had launched into the garden in search of other adventures.

Nobody knows where Mina is now!

THE TRAFFIC LIGHT THAT GIVES THE COLORS

Once there was a traffic light that he was tired of doing the same thing every day.

He was tired of always following the rule: first red, then green, finally orange. Every day the same colors, the same cars and the same scenes: the minibus loaded with screaming children went to school at 7:45 am, the old man who went to buy the newspaper on a bicycle whistling, Rosina's mother put on lipstick when the traffic light was red, Paolo's father whizzing by in his shiny new car to get to the office on time.

Every now and then something new happened to enliven her routine: one time the grandma Ada hadn't noticed that the traffic light was red she had to brake suddenly to avoid an accident with Tobia, the town baker, leaving two black braking marks on the asphalt. Or that time when Tino the farmer was carrying a wagon full of grapes to go to the social cellar: suddenly the box was opened and all the grapes ended up on the road blocking traffic.

The traffic light had enjoyed it, yes, but he was looking for the thrill.
So, one day he rebelled! He decided to give the colors! Yes, yes, you got it right, the colors!

It began with the green: quiet motorists passed by, but suddenly, just before the pedestrian crossing, the red one clicked and confused who were forced to brake sharply. Or, immediately after the red triggered the orange and the drivers did not know if they could start slowly or stay still.

One day even later the orange turned green and the motorists set off again, but then suddenly the red one arrived and various rear-end collisions were created on the road which caused the police and firefighters to intervene. And the traffic light was laughing under his breath while enjoying the shows.

For their part, motorists no longer knew what to expect from the traffic lights, there was always the fear that a new color would suddenly take off. Many, to avoid accidents, took other roads, lengthening their path.

Eventually the traffic light was sent to the repair shop and replaced with a more reliable one.

THE WITCH DISPETTINA

Among the many witches that exist in the world, there is one who loves to mischief and mess around. This little witch is called Dispettina and no one knows why, but she focuses her mischief on children. Particularly on those who go to school.

She makes herself small and hides in the classrooms: from that position she can see everything without being noticed. She takes out his wand and "zac", with a little spell she makes small mistakes appear in the children's notebooks.

One day Martina, a diligent and always prepared child, was carrying out an operation on the notebook, taking great care to calculate the numbers correctly. She writes the result and "zac", Dispettina puts a hand in it and changes the number 9 to the number 7. When the teacher corrected the notebooks, she was surprised to find a mistake in Martina's notebook.

Another day, it happened to Tommaso that, while he was writing a dictation, he missed a few letters, because Dispettina had a hand in it, and he found a bad vote from the teacher. In fact, in the notebook it was written: "The little dog Billy was running after a spider that had tree legs. He did not notice that there was a hedgehog and he stung himself with his quilt ". How many mistakes!

And Dispettina laughs every time she does one of her jokes. When she finds out that we have done enough damage in that class, she goes to another class and performs his spells.

So if these inexplicable mistakes have happened to you too, know that it is all the fault of Dispettina who has set foot in your class.

THE MOUSE OF THE TEETH

In every family we know there is a little mouse of the teeth, that is, that little mouse that when some child loses his teeth around the age of 5, he takes it away and adds it to his collection and in exchange leaves a penny to the child to thank him.

Ettore was five and a half years old and his first tooth was about to come off completely. He did not have much faith in these strange stories about tooth mice and did not like to go around toothless, so, he kept the dangling tooth jealously guarded in his mouth.

He avoided playing with other children, running and throwing the ball for fear that a few shots would make him leave his teeth. He just didn't understand why it was necessary to change these teeth!

One night, however, the little mouse, tired of waiting for Ettore's tooth, since he had other children on the list who were about to lose a tooth, decided to intervene directly: while the child was sleeping, he slowly approached the bed, slowly opened the mouth and took that tooth without even making too much effort, since it was almost completely detached. He left in a hurry, leaving a penny under Ettore's pillow.

In the morning, Ettore got up to go to school, went to the bathroom and while he was washing his face he noticed that something was wrong. The tooth was gone !!! What if he had swallowed it? God, his first tooth had disappeared without his noticing, what a bummer!

While he was on the bed desperate because he had lost his tooth, he saw a small glow coming from under the pillow. It was the penny left by the mouse! Then it was true that there was a tooth mouse! He had never seen such a shiny coin, really special!

With that penny he consoled himself and immediately began to feel the state of his teeth, because he couldn't wait for the mouse to bring him the next penny.

THE MAGIC HAT

Merlin has a new hat: it is pointed and has gold stars on red velvet.

The little wizard walks happily down the street when he is hit by a violent gust of wind. The wind blows the hat off his head and pulls him over the fence.

- Stop! -cries Merlin.

What a misfortune! The hat ended up in the garden of the Iron Tooth witch, which everyone calls in that way because of her iron canine. Everyone avoids her because she is always in a bad mood.

- What do I do now? - Merlin complains. Should he leave his hat in the witch's hands?

Now he's in a bad mood too. She reluctantly climbs the fence.

His dress, however, remains entangled.

The little wizard squirms and tries to break free.

- Stupid fence! - he shouts furiously.

Suddenly he hears a loud laugh: Iron Tooth is standing in front of him!

- What are you doing here? - the witch chuckles.

- I have to get my hat back. - Merlin mumbles.

- You're all disheveled! - laughs the witch, -You're funny! It was a life that I didn't laugh so much!

- And is it a good thing? - asks Merlin.

- Of course it is! - answers Iron Tooth.

The witch helps Merlin free himself and returns his hat.

- Would you like some chocolate with cream? - asks Iron Tooth, - It's the reward for making me laugh.

- Sure, thanks! - replies the little wizard. How lucky, not only did

Merlin get his hat back, but he also found a new friend.

THE HIDDEN HATCH

On a dark and silent night Nico and Max, without making the slightest noise, got out of bed and went into the living room. They lifted the carpet and found the mysterious trap door Dad always talked about. They were not allowed to open it and this sparked their curiosity.

The two brothers turned on the flashlight and walked slowly down the stairs without being heard by their sleeping parents. Pointing the light, they found a large garage in front of them where there were all kinds of machinery with pipes, pumps, small tanks. They looked at them carefully, one by one, without understanding what kind of machinery they were.

Continuing to search the whole room, they found a strange photo hanging on the wall with some gentlemen with top hats proudly holding some sort of document in their hands. Who were those gentlemen? What was written in that document?

They left there with no answer and decided to continue investigating the next day.

They rested everything in perfect order and went back to bed, but without being able to sleep: they had too many unanswered questions to be able to sleep, too many suppositions crowded their minds.

The next day, as if nothing had happened the previous night, they had breakfast, went to school and meanwhile continued to think about the mysterious discovery in their home. At that point, the only thing to do was to face the parents directly and ask them for all the explanations of what they had seen. At dinner they broached the subject. The father knew that sooner or later he would have to deal with the subject, so he began to tell:

- Dear guys, you must know that your grandfather was a very curious and rebellious scientist! All those machines were at him and we have to keep them hidden because he had discovered something very important that he couldn't complete because he left us earlier.

Grandpa had discovered how to double and triple the food, yes, you got it right! Putting, for example, an apple in one of the machines, we can get two and even three.

The two brothers were stunned and couldn't believe their ears! What a special grandfather they had! What a wonderful find!

They kept the secret for a long time, until they made known to everyone the discovery of their grandfather, after having worked extensively on it in the following previous months.

STICKERS COME TO LIFE

In Martin's bedroom, there are tons of stickers that he has stuck everywhere: on the wardrobe, on the door, on the desk and even on the glass. Martin loves stickers, he likes to stick them even on notebooks and his mother gives him some at every good occasion. He likes having a room full of colors and characters, he feels less alone, since he is an only child and always has someone to keep him company, both day and night. Sometimes he also talks to them, with Superman, Batman and Ninja Turtles.

There is one thing you don't know and neither does Martin know: every morning, when the child goes to school in his room, magical things happen. The stickers come to life, they detach from the walls and furniture and play, talk, jump, in short, a real revolution happens in that room.

The Hulk boss as soon as he hears the door close say to everyone gets animated. Minnie and Mickey Mouse have the opportunity to hang out for a while, the Ninja Turtles train by jumping from the bed to the nightstand and sometimes they remain attached to the window pane and it's up to Hulk to go and detach them. Superman does flight tests and occasionally saves some girls in danger, while Spiderman slowly descends from the ceiling to check the tightness of his web.

You must know that Martin knows exactly where he has attached each of his stikers and for this reason, one fine day on his return from school, he found it very strange that Captain America had ended up right on the head of his bed! He thought about it and was convinced that his mother, by cleaning up the room, had dropped the super hero and hung him up where she had found a place. But a few days later even Harry Potter had ended up somewhere else! He decides to ask his mother, but she denied having hung up his stickers. So Martin began to investigate thoroughly: what was going on in that room?

One day he took the internal camera that his father placed near the entrance door to see if thieves entered during their absence. He went to school and on his way back, eager to check what the camera had recorded, he locked himself in the studio with the excuse of having to do a research for the school and ... surprise! The recording showed all of his stickers peeling off the walls and coming to life! What a wonderful find for Martin! He knew his stickers were special!

At that point he decided to talk to all his stickers:

- Dear characters, I know that when I go to school you wake up and start to break away! I ask you a courtesy: by now I have discovered your secret, therefore, detach yourself freely whenever you want, even when I am here with you, so we can play together and get to know each other better.

Timidly. The mighty Hulk raised his thumb in approval and gave the signal for all stickers to peel off. Martin was so happy with the company of his stickers that he no longer felt alone.

Lightning Source UK Ltd.
Milton Keynes UK
UKHW020814020321
379644UK00001B/33